CW00408185

**How to navigate the changes and
uncertainties of young adulthood**

"IT'S TIME TO LOOK UP!"

Erin Lee Gray

IT'S TIME TO LOOK UP
Copyright © 2021 by Erin Lee Gray

ISBN: 978-1-915223-02-9

Main translation in use: Scripture quotations taken from the THE HOLY BIBLE, NEW INTERNATIONAL VERSION®, NIV® Copyright © 1973, 1978, 1984, 2011 by Biblica, Inc.® Used by permission. All rights reserved worldwide.

Scripture quotations marked MSG are taken from *THE MESSAGE*, Copyright © 1993, 2002, 2018 by Eugene H. Peterson. Used by permission of NavPress. All rights reserved. Represented by Tyndale House Publishers, Inc.

Good News Translation® (Today's English Version, Second Edition) Copyright © 1992 American Bible Society. All rights reserved.

The Christian Standard Bible. Copyright © 2017 by Holman Bible Publishers. Used by permission. Christian Standard Bible®, and CSB® are federally registered trademarks of Holman Bible Publishers, all rights reserved.

Published by

Maurice Wylie Media
Your Inspirational Christian Publisher

Publisher's statement: Throughout this book the love for our God is such that whenever we refer to Him we honour with capitals. On the other hand, when referring to the devil, we refuse to acknowledge him with any honour to the point of violating grammatical rule and withholding capitalisation.

For more information visit
www.MauriceWylieMedia.com

CONTENTS

DEDICATION

To my Mum and Dad, who have always believed in me, encouraged me, and allowed me to pursue my dreams. I wouldn't be who I am today without their wisdom, guidance and love. Thank you. I love you both.

ACKNOWLEDGEMENTS

A BIG thank you to...

Mum - for showing me what it means to love selflessly, demonstrating what unshakable faith looks like and how to have joy in every season. You elegantly display beauty inside and out.

Dad - for your resilience, your strength, and your ambition. Thank you for teaching me about being intentional, for sharing your wisdom and for always having an answer to my weird and wonderful questions.

My closest - Rebekah, for showing me what true friendship looks like, for demonstrating trust, loyalty and love. Eve, for encouraging me in all I do and always bringing that extra bit of joy. Robyn, for always being there for me and always seeing the best in me in every season. I'm incredibly grateful for your input into my life and for the many memories shared.

My family - both biologically and relationally—You mean the world to me, and I'm forever grateful for the laughs, hugs and memories shared. You make me feel cherished and loved.

My grandparents - for the legacy of faith you all left. Thank you for the love you implanted in my parents and the foundation of faith you all built. I now stand on your legacy and seek to keep on building upon that foundation of faith and love into this next generation.

My Saviour Jesus Christ - for captivating my heart. I will forever be grateful for your faithfulness, grace, kindness, unfailing love and the beautiful reality that your promises are true. All praise be to the Father.

ENDORSEMENTS

Erin informs us that the average person can have up to 60,000 thoughts a day and 80% of these are negative. In this book she reminds us "we were never meant to carry the weight of the world" but she points us repeatedly to the one who does.

Drawing on her own experience, she gives practical advice on how we can guard our minds and enjoy life with freedom and peace. Erin has not written from a pedestal of perfection but as a peer who has wrestled with some of the potential pitfalls of moving through teenage years into adulthood. I have known Erin since she was a young teen and know that she speaks with integrity and has lived out her own faith consistently.

Phil Hills, Chief Executive of Teen Challenge UK and Vice President of Global Teen Challenge.

Erin is one of the most consistent Christians I know. Her perspective on young adulthood in this book helps me understand why... mind you, she shares wisdom for people of all ages. It is so easy, in this fast-paced, changing world, where we are surrounded with negativity, comparison and uncertainty, to feel out of control and be consumed with worry. In this book, Erin wants to have a chat with you and share how she has found hope.

Her refreshing vulnerability, honesty, clarity and conviction of faith will help you realise there is more in this life. So, why not 'look up' and see the hope that can only come from a life-centred upon Jesus! I am so thankful that Erin has written this book and I pray you are blessed through it.

Philip Kerr, Co-Founder of Crown Jesus Ministries and Executive Pastor at Dundonald Elim Church.

Erin gives such a refreshing insight into life as a young adult. She shares her experiences openly and honestly, that we all can hold our hands up in agreement with what she has faced; but she shares her story with such hope, each time always pointing to Jesus as the solution to our problems. Her words are gentle & kind, showing Grace in every chapter, whilst also offering wise & practical help. These pages are littered with words of Truth & Hope.

David Hume, Youth Pastor at Dundonald Elim Church.

This is a book by a young adult for young adults. It's packed full of wisdom, truth and hope. Erin's words weave a tapestry that will inspire young adults to remember that God holds them through all the challenges that they face and that God's purposes for them liberate them into the greatest adventure of all- the life of faith. I can't commend it enough. A terrific book by a remarkable young woman.'

Rev. Malcolm Duncan FRSA, Lead Pastor of Dundonald Elim Church; Theologian-in-Residence for Spring Harvest and Essential Christian; New Horizons board member; Author; Broadcaster and Blogger.

INTRODUCTION

Hey friend,

I am so glad that you have decided to pick up this book, and I really hope that, as you read through the words that are on the pages to follow, you will know that you are loved, experience a sense of peace in your heart, and understand the important practice of looking up when things around you seem out of your control.

As you read please don't see these concepts, thoughts or words and detach them from an individual but take this book as an intimate conversation between two friends.

There was a time in my late teens that I felt like everything in my life was shifting and all I wanted was for it to stand still. I wish someone had told me not to fret but to actually engage, experience and embrace all the changes because, in spite of the unknown, there was so much beauty that came from that season. That's why I'm chatting to you here, to share these thoughts with you in the hope that you too would find beauty in the season you are in.

Everything I have written in this book is built upon my faith in Jesus but whether you are reading this as a Christian or not I would love to share with you some practical steps that have helped me in the hope that they will help you as well, to give you some insight into the life of Jesus so that you would feel encouraged and find hope in this stage of life and every one thereafter.

May this book offer you a hand of advice or guidance in both the big and little moments and even those little moments that feel big.

Remember, no matter what you're going through, *It's Time to Look Up!*

CHAPTER 1
WHOSE WEIGHT ARE YOU CARRYING?

As I write this book, our world is still in the midst of recurring lockdowns and uncertainties surrounding coronavirus. In this season, it can be easy to focus on the negative and uncertainty and become overwhelmed with the fear that the media is trying to instil in us surrounding safety, health and the unknown with regards to the future economy, education system and job security. To be honest, it is a time where it would be easy to freak out and, if it had happened when I was in my teens, I would be freaking out, being someone who was naturally drawn to worry, which then grew into fear and anxiety in my late teenage years. This was a regular occurrence until I hit a point that I knew I couldn't keep going the way I was going and realised that my focus had to shift. I had to learn to take control of my thoughts while asking myself, "How on earth do I do that?" You may be feeling the same way, feeling overcome by worry or numbed by fear but you don't have to stay there.

I personally had to come to a place of realisation that I couldn't do it in my own strength. Overcoming worry and fear in that particular season (which I will chat about later) wasn't an easy process as you can imagine; it was a spiritual and mental battle for a long time. Worry specifically still likes to creep in from time to time even when it's not welcome, but where worry used to be my natural reaction to many situations, it now only tends to raise its head in the midst of more serious scenarios. I am overcoming! All glory to God that worry and fear **no longer** has its grasp over me but with that being said, it doesn't come as a shock to me that young people seem to be the ones struggling most throughout this last year or so. It can seem hopeless, confusing and isolating.

I personally know how fear can grow and consume your mind. Like a small flame that begins to grow the more you feed it with wood, so does fear. It makes you feel anything but safe. So whilst not disregarding how you feel, in the midst of that fear, allow the security of the Father's presence and His peace to override the things the world may be throwing at you. Begin to train your mind to combat each negative or detrimental thought with His Word and what He says about you. Let the certainty of who He is outweigh the uncertainty that may be around you. Our Saviour is the same yesterday, today and forever, and He isn't surprised by how you feel or what you are facing. He is a BIG God, and He has got you right in the palm of His hand.

I think we can all agree that 2020 was a year that most definitely had its challenges and, whilst I don't want to diminish the sorrow and confusion it brought, in the midst of it all there have also been many victories, blessings and transformations in people's lives. We have been given this gift of time. The question is, what are we going to do with it? I believe this last year or so has helped us to realign our focus, to enjoy making memories with our families, to be more intentional with our time, and to be thankful for the little things that we may have previously taken for granted.

Conversations have been had, coffee dates have become more valued, and being outdoors became a beautiful escape, but not only that, people have expanded and grown upon skills and talents, taken up hobbies, built new relationships, and dreamt new dreams. I encourage you to think over this past year and write down three things that you are thankful for in this season whether you think it's big or small. Let me help you.

My 3 are:

1. Having the time to be more intentional

2. Trying new things and taking on new hobbies

3. My family

Your 3 are:

1. ....

2. ....

3. ....

As I said, it's time to retrain our thinking, and one way to do that is to switch our mentality to one of thankfulness. Being thankful doesn't have to start with the big things, but it begins when we approach life with a grateful heart for our surroundings, our connections and our life. There is always something we can be thankful for.

> To live a life with a thankful attitude we must realign our thought patterns in a direction towards hope and positivity.

To bring light into moments of darkness and to reveal that hope in what can seem like a frustrating season can be transformative and life changing.

I don't know if you have ever seen *The Chronicles of Narnia*[1] but where they were surrounded in winter, there was a light that brought hope to Narnia through the faith of one little girl called Lucy. She not only found the light, but she brought light to the lives of those she encountered and had faith in the purpose that Aslan (symbolic of Jesus) brought. They were stuck in darkness but with a little bit of hope, boldness and belief, the light overcame the darkness.

In all that the world is going through, you and I are going to be fed negative press, hear countless opinions, and listen to many perspectives of what to believe, how to think, and what you should be engaging with. You may have heard it said that "we are the most connected generation yet the loneliest that society has ever been." But you were never meant to take in and handle every piece of information thrown at you through social media, the news, and the opinions of those around you. It's a lot to ingest, especially when the news normally reports the worst and creates a sense of uncertainty above all else. The truth is that you were never meant to carry the weight of the world. Our minds can become so overwhelmed due to the sheer amount we are consuming through our screens.

So let me ask, "How are you feeding your mind?"

Is your main source of food coming from the headlines?

Are you feeding off the success or downfalls or other people's lives on social media? Are you comparing aspects of your life to others around you?

If we allow all these inlets to be the main things that fill our minds, no wonder we can feel overwhelmed and worried about the future.

It is important to note that being informed of world affairs and having social media for fun, business and connection is beneficial; they definitely have their positives and their place. However, when we allow the media and the opinions of others to become our main input of information, we end up allowing too many negative voices to take a seat in our minds, sometimes clouding our judgement and perspective. If our peace is taken, our thoughts can be disrupted, and fear and uncertainty can seek to overcome us.

Don't let fear take over from the light that can be found, because on top of the beauty that can be embraced in our everyday and in our relationships with one another, there is a Saviour who is above all and His name is Jesus. He died on a cross, but He rose from the dead so that we can live in His peace and have His presence. He defeated death and sin so that you and I did not have to carry all of life's heavy stuff. Allow Him to carry your load and rest in His embrace.

He seeks for you to live a life of freedom **in and through** Him.

Whether you believe Jesus died on the cross for you or not, I can guarantee that you have probably thought about there being a deeper meaning to life. Why do I say this? Because I believe that there is something in us all that knows there is more or at least hopes for more. We as human beings desire to be filled, to feel wanted, loved and seen, and each of these needs and desires of the human heart are only completely fulfilled and satisfied through Jesus. So bring your questions, your brokenness, your hurts, your failures, and all of the in-between to Him and let Him lift your burdens. Let Him breathe a breath of fresh air into your life daily because God created you with purpose and seeks for you to look to Him for clarity, love, acceptance, redemption and freedom.

With that in mind, I would love to share with you this beautiful analogy: Footprints in the Sand:

Footprints in the Sand[2]

"One night I dreamed I was walking along the beach with the Lord. Many scenes from my life flashed across the sky. In each scene I noticed footprints in the sand. Sometimes there were two sets of footprints, other times there was one. This bothered me because I noticed that during the low periods of my life, when I was suffering from anguish, sorrow or defeat, I could see only one set of footprints, so I said to the Lord, 'You promised me, Lord, that if I followed You, You would walk with me always. But I have noticed that during the most trying periods of life there has only been one set of footprints in the sand. Why, when I needed You the most, have You not been there for me?' The Lord replied, 'The years when you have seen only one set of footprints, my child, is when I carried you.'"

A beautiful picture and reminder that God will never leave you or forsake you. He is with you always, walking with you and carrying you. I encourage you to take a step back from the noise and be still in Him.

CHAPTER 2
The Father heart of God

Something that has really been on my heart for the last couple of years and has helped me to realign my focus when combating the anxious thoughts as well as navigating different seasons and circumstances is to physically and spiritually look up. There is a song that implanted this idea in the power of looking up, and it is called *"Look up, Child"* by Lauren Daigle.[3] The first verse goes like this:

> *"Where are You now when darkness seems to win?*
> *Where are You now when the world is crumbling?*
> *Oh I, I-I-I, I hear You say, I hear You say.*
> *'Look up, child.' Hey. 'Look up, child.' Hey."*

In the uncertainty of this world and the confusion that can surround us, it is important to remember that God is in control, that He is a good, good **Father**, and that sometimes all we need to do is LOOK UP! He is always ready with arms open wide for you to run into His presence. Rest in His sovereignty, authority and love.

Something that is so beautiful about this song is that it refers to us as children who can look up to not only the King but to our Father. We can come to our Heavenly Father like a child should be able to come to an earthly father. God chose you, yes you, and He wants a relationship with you. He's always there with open arms to embrace you with His love.

Now I know that the word ***father*** can bring different connotations for different people. You might have been blessed, as I have been, with a loving, caring and encouraging father and, if you have, please don't take that for granted. But I am also aware there are many individuals who don't know their father, or they resent, hate or are fearful of their father. This can bring disappointment and/or leave a void in one's life.

You may be someone who has experienced a "performance-based" love from a father; according to what you deliver, love is given. Then there are "abusive fathers," those who may have verbally, physically or sexually abusive. You may have had a father who constantly compared you to your siblings or didn't give you the time of day, being more concerned with other things. Or maybe your father was absent either by choice or by a misfortunate, painful or agonising circumstance. First, I want to say I am so sorry if you haven't had the experience of a loving father but please hear me when I say it shouldn't define who you are. We must take our experiences and learn from them. Give yourself a bit of grace and learn to swap the season of abuse, hurt or isolation for a lifetime of purpose, fulfilment and peace. You deserve love.

If you struggle to comprehend this type of love, please read this prayer I have written for you:

> *Dear God, I pray directly into the life of this reader. I ask that you would meet them where they are right now, whether that be in a season of pain, uncertainty, confusion, restoration or frustration. Let Your peace transcend into their heart. Bring forth freedom from bondage, speak life into sorrow, provide comfort for the broken-hearted, and may the beautiful mercy and grace of God be evident in their life. Jesus, may this reader know they are loved, that they are worthy and beautiful in Your eyes. Thank You for dying on the cross for me and for them. Thank You for Your power and sovereignty. And thank You that, even though You are so vast, You care about what we care about. Jesus, help them to walk in all You have for them and may Your joy be thier strength. In the beautiful name of Jesus, Amen.*

No earthly father can equate to the beauty of the Heavenly Father but, without that positive earthly representation of love, support and protection, it can be hard to accept that there is a Heavenly Father who loves you let alone wants a relationship with you. In that regard, having a good, earthly father can make the concept of God as our "Father" an easier one to accept, although it can be one that is much harder to grasp. **Accepting and grasping** are two very different things. I can accept and grasp that my earthly father loves me, but when I try to comprehend that the Creator of all things loves and cares for me, it can be hard to grasp the reality of it. Yet the reality is that He loves you too.

How can we as imperfect people even think of coming before a perfect God? It's hard to wrap your head around but the answer is simply JESUS. It is because of Jesus that we can come before our Heavenly Father free of shame, fear and condemnation. We don't have to come to Him with our heads hanging low in shame, but we can come spotless before the Father when we humble ourselves before Him. He isn't a Father that will slap our wrists when we do wrong but One who will put His hand beneath our chins and lift our heads up high to have our gaze fixed on Him. Let Him take your shame, your hurt and your pain. Hand it over in surrender to Him. Jesus already carried it all on the cross so you don't have to carry it anymore. Let the Heavenly Father wrap you in His grace and unfailing love.

If you are still struggling to comprehend the love God has for and towards you read this collection of verses from the Bible to describe the Heavenly Father's love for you and His thoughts towards you at all times.

"Jesus said, 'Let the little children come to me, and do not hinder them, for the kingdom of heaven belongs to such as these'" (Matthew 19:14).

"'And I will be a father to you, and you shall be sons and daughters to Me,' says the Lord Almighty" (2 Corinthians 6:18).

"So you are no longer a slave, but God's child; and since you are his child, God has made you also an heir" (Galatians 4:7).

"For God so loved the world that He gave His one and only Son, so that everyone who believes in him will not perish but have eternal life" (John 3:16).

"Now a slave has no permanent place in the family, but a son belongs to it forever. So if the Son sets you free, you will be free indeed" (John 8:35-36).

I hope that you will experience restoration from God's Word and let the truth of who He says you are override and speak above what has been spoken over you.

In a book I read recently by Louie Giglio called *Not Forsaken,*[4] he writes, *"No matter what has happened on this side of eternity between you and your dad; you are not forsaken by God."* He wants to be your Father. He wants you to live in abundance, to have hope, feel safe, protected, adored and to know you belong. He wants you to grow, learn and become all you were called to be. So please grasp the truth of what the Heavenly Father says about you over everything else.

As a kid I had no doubt that my dad was the strongest man I knew, I had full and complete trust in him. I knew he would pick me up when I fell, take my hand when I needed guidance, and always wanted what was best for me. I'm so grateful that the same is true today—always loving me and looking out for me, a blessing beyond words. But no matter how much my dad loves me, the love your Heavenly Father has for you is so much more palpable, divine and true.[5] You just need to come to Him with childlike faith and trust in who He is.

Look up, child, from the worries of this world and the confusion of your current circumstance, for He is with you. He is there to lead and guide you, to hold your hand in every circumstance—good and bad. He is right behind you, encouraging and protecting you from harm. With the faith of a child, look up to the Father, for He has got you, and He is never letting go.

Keeping in mind this reminder to look up, let's dive into some of the changes and challenges in **young adulthood**.

CHAPTER 3
Trusting in God and His Word

Whether you are just entering into young adulthood, smack bang in the centre of your twenties, or slipping into older adulthood, this season of life is full of many alterations to your current "normality." You will have a lot to figure out that involves you stepping into new things and experiencing change. I want to talk to you about some of those things that I personally have experienced. And trust me, I am not the fountain of all knowledge, but as I share some of my thoughts and experiences, I hope that they will bring some help to your situation and remind you that you aren't on your own nor are you the only one who feels the way you do.

There are so many changes in life, especially throughout your teens and twenties. Few people talk about them, and when they do the emphasis is on events that happen or goals to reach. But what about how to emotionally, mentally and spiritually prepare yourself or how to practically approach this stage of life along with having the right mindset?

There are many shifts in routine and changes in lifestyle that happen. There are changes in education, relationships, finances, and much more—all of which require a bit of a shake-up in our mentality and thinking.

However, before I talk about these areas of change that you will most definitely come across in your young adulthood, I want to explain the importance of posturing ourselves towards Jesus. First and foremost, we need to focus on His truth, His life, death and resurrection, and His love. We have to establish a firm foundation in our Saviour, not only to give us a stable ground to build our lives upon, but also to give Him His rightful place, to be at the centre of our lives and in the midst of every decision and circumstance.

"For from him and through him and for him are all things. To him be the glory forever, Amen" Romans 11:36.

Our posture needs to turn towards our Heavenly Father, our Creator. For when we fall upon our knees and lift our eyes to Him, we place ourselves in a humbled posture of grace toward the Saviour. With eyes fixed upon Jesus as a child's gaze follows their father's, may we look to Him for guidance, wisdom, discernment, strength, hope and, most importantly, love.

As you build your life upon the Lord and His truths, you position yourself on an unshakeable foundation.

A daily decision to put your trust in God can bring peace to your mind and rest to your soul.

This, combined with the consistent renewal of His Spirit in you, will fill your life with hope and your heart with love. So before you continue to read through these chapters of ideas, scenarios and seasons which I personally believe in or have been through, posture yourself towards the Lord. Allow Him to transform your thinking, renew your mind and speak to your heart.

"Above all else, guard your heart, for everything you do flows from it" Proverbs 4:23.

You may be thinking, how do I posture myself towards the Lord if I don't know Him, trust Him, or feel like I'm in a place to even know where to start? Well, the simple but hard answer would be, have FAITH. I know, it's easier said than done, right? Let's dive a bit deeper into trust because once you know the **One** you are trusting **in** is trustworthy, it's much easier to have faith in Him and to posture yourself towards Him.

Our human nature is to only trust those who have earned our trust, or alternatively to only trust those we really know so then the question is raised, "Do I trust in God?"

If you even glimpse at the Bible let alone read it in depth you will see the provision and promises of God throughout. He is trustworthy and true. He never breaks or goes back on a promise. A prime example of this would be Noah.

Whether from a felt board in school and putting the animals in pairs or if you read it for yourself as a grown up, we all probably know Noah. In Genesis 6.9-10 we read that *"Noah was a man of integrity in his community. Noah walked with God"* (MSG). So you can imagine the community's reaction when a respected and noble man started to build a massive boat with no sign of rain on its way. I imagine he experienced some amount of scoffing and an immense array of insults. Yet because Noah **walked with God**, He knew Him and put His trust in Him. -

And as you continue to read, you will see that the flood did, in fact, come just as God said it would and destroyed everything outside of it. God then made a promise to Noah, a covenant between Him and man—one which we still see the representation and evidence of today in our skies in the form of a rainbow—this beautiful promise from God showing the relationship and trust between a man of

God and a promise-keeping Father. Even when it's not easy to trust in Him and it's difficult to put that trust into action, the more we get to know Him, spend time with Him and walk with Him, the more we will begin to trust Him.

Now I understand that it can be daunting to put your trust in what some would call an "unseen God" and to no longer be consumed by life's challenges. However, when you begin to gain the perspective that everything is in His hands and control to begin with, it can ignite a spark within you to create that process of change in your heart. You can begin the process towards experiencing the freedom that He longed for you to have.

When Jesus died and rose again, He not only paid the ultimate price to save our souls for eternity, but His sacrifice meant and still means that we can live in total freedom and truly live life from a place of love, acceptance and complete fullness. Not freedom in the sense of doing whatever you want when you want, but freedom from fear, doubt, not feeling good enough or accepted, a freedom from trying to prove yourself or doubting your self-worth. Jesus believed you were worth dying for, so you are enough as you are—broken, weary, hurt, frustrated, lacking in confidence. Trying to wrap your head around the fact that Jesus loves you so much can sound too good to be true but it's the most beautiful gift, and if you accept Him as your Lord and Saviour, you can truly live in that freedom and trust in His promises.

Trusting in Him is a daily decision, a daily rhythm to get our hearts and minds in the right place, and it starts with posturing ourselves towards the Father. I'm not going to lie. I have found it really tough to shift my thinking to truly trust in God. I am someone who likes to feel like I am in control and can handle all that life has to offer or throw at me all on my own, but the truth is I can't do everything on my own, nor can I control everything. My mind used to wander from scenario to scenario trying to work things out, to fix things, change things, predict things, and it just sent me into a spiral of worry and frustration.

Ironically, my favourite verse growing up was from Proverbs 3:5-6, *"Trust in the Lord with all of your heart and lean not on your own understanding. In all your ways acknowledge him and he will direct your paths."* It still is one of my favourite passages but as a teen I learnt this and spoke it over myself.

This was a start but I kept these words as head knowledge for far too long before recognising the need to transfer it to heart knowledge. I was too focused on what I thought I knew to be true and was believing every thought that came to my mind. Our thoughts are incredibly important as they give us discernment which can lead to wisdom, but if you take your perspective and your understanding ONLY, it will not lead to a lasting life. You cannot trust what YOU think above what God says. In fact, it has been found that the average person has about 12,000-60,000 thoughts per day of which 80% are negative and 95% are exactly the same repetitive thoughts as the day before.[6] I think that shows that we are 1) overthinkers and 2) negative individuals.

So just like I did, it's time to release that grasp of control, and let God be the one directing and leading you.

Take your own discernment and God's Word to bring about transformation to your thinking. Once your thoughts begin to be transformed, they soon flow to your heart. I was so focused on my understanding of things that I was trying to work out and direct my own paths instead of fixing my focus on my Father.

> I needed to hand over control to the One who was already in control, to trust in His understanding and believe that He had me and my life in the palm of His hands.

This doesn't mean times of worry don't still feature in my life, but they no longer control me like they used to and, honestly, it took me years to get to the frame of mind that I have now. A lot of the transformation came from doing things afraid. Through the grace and love of God, good books, my parents' wisdom, and learning to focus on what I could control while handing over what I couldn't to Jesus, I slowly but surely began to have more and more confidence in my Creator and who He created me to be.

It's easy to let the worry override the trust, especially because most people around you will normally emit a worry mentality about something. As you hear, listen and take in that worry, you can subconsciously begin to worry along with them. It's one of the many reasons it's incredibly important to fill your mind with the Word of God and positivity, so that when your own thoughts or others' thoughts begin to fill your mind, you have God's Word of hope, life and truth to override it.

Imagine a tennis ball launcher and one by one the tennis balls get thrown your way, each one representing a negative voice …

"You will never be enough."
"Will I ever feel loved?"
"Did you see the news?"
"What do you think will happen if …?"
"Don't you worry about …?"
"It's all very unknown. Isn't it scary?"
"What if I'm not accepted?"

... each of these either coming from your own mind or those around you. Now imagine being opposite the machine without a racket. Each ball that gets thrown towards you either gets hit repeatedly or you attempt to dodge their aim. You will end up getting bruised and hurt or become exhausted from running away from each one. What if you had a racket? With this device, you would be equipped to hit the balls out of your way. The racket doesn't stop the tennis balls from being thrown at you, but it gives you the tool and the ability to deflect them, preventing serious injury and training you and making you grow stronger. The racket can represent God's Word, His truth and His promises. Having His truth and guidance as a positive reflex to negativity helps hit away what could be going through your mind and what others try to throw your way. Use His Word to counteract negative, unproductive and hurtful words that are thrown at you, for His Word has power.

John 1:1-5 says, *"In the beginning was the Word, and the Word was with God, and the Word was God. He was with God in the beginning. Through him all things were made; without him nothing was made that has been made. In him was life, and that life was the light of all mankind. The light shines in the darkness, and the darkness has not overcome it."*

Many times, we hear how God sent His One and only Son into the world to save us and to redeem us but following that we often hear about the instructions, the healings and all of the miracles and actions that partook in Jesus' life and how that impacts us today. Now all of these things are of incredible importance, and we should always seek to learn about Jesus, His life and all He said and did.[7] However, in a devotion I recently read it said, *"Jesus did not come to merely deliver a message from God—He Himself is the message."*

Jesus didn't only appear in the New Testament but there is evidence of His presence throughout the entirety of Scripture. As John states in John 1:1, *"In the beginning was the Word, the Word was WITH God and the Word WAS God."*

John began his gospel echoing the heart and being of God while simultaneously emphasising the beauty and essence of Christ.

We are witnessing a man who was one of Jesus' best friends write about His story and character, but we also see a description of the intentionality and significance of WHO HE WAS AND IS AND IS TO COME. Without this becoming a theological lesson or debate I would like to portray to you that the Jesus who was in the beginning, who is evident throughout history and is still with us today, cares for and loves you, yes you! When He came into this world He brought us a message of hope, a promise that can never be broken, that anyone who believes in Him shall not perish but have everlasting life. The devotional I was referring to went on further to describe Jesus as "a tangible love letter from God." He came into this world sent from above as a gift of love. This letter of love was written throughout history and lived out in the day-to-day life and actions of Jesus which then echoed into humanity.

Have you ever received a love letter? Whether from a friend, a spouse, a boyfriend/girlfriend or a family member, when someone takes the time to write down their thoughts and feelings for you or towards you it can warm your heart. It makes you feel loved, accepted and cherished. I personally love writing letters to people. It's such an intentional way of saying how you feel, to bring to someone your gratitude for them, and to let them know how much they mean to you. So whether you have or haven't received a love letter, you most definitely have received one from your Creator—the most beautiful message of love that is above all of the others you may have received. Jesus is God's expression of love to you, one that is so deep it's eternal and unshakeable.

In the midst of anything you are going through, remind yourself of His love and the love He sent to this world for you and me to live freely and abundantly. The things of this world can so easily try to distract us or draw our attention from the giver of life, yet He is the only one that allows us to truly live. As I go into these next chapters and talk through the many things you will come across or face as a young adult, first and foremost build your life upon the truth of Jesus and trust in Him.

CHAPTER 4
WHEN THINGS DON'T GO AS YOU PLANNED

One of the first things you will realise as a young adult is that nothing ever really goes the way you had planned or turns out the way you think it would have. When I think back to when I was 15, I imagined that within the next ten years I would have my career sorted, be married, have kids, have all of my money in order, have a house, and all of the in-between. The naiveté of my teenage self, thinking everything has to and will come to pass by a certain age and within **my** particular timeframe. So just a little additional reminder that no matter what age you are, you are exactly where you need to be.

That's the thing about your twenties. With so many things changing, it's inevitable that everyone will be moving at a different pace. Some may have had a passion to become a nurse from childhood whilst their best friend still has no idea what their passions are at 22. You may have found your childhood sweetheart and love of your life at 16 but your friend may not have met the one yet and they are 26. Regardless of what specific stage you are at, you are learning, growing and becoming the wonderful you. So a piece of advice that will last a lifetime:

Stop comparing yourself to others. Stay in your lane, focus on your path, work towards your goals, and cheer each other on as you experience this wonderful thing called life.

For me I didn't always know what I wanted to do with my life, especially in terms of a career but I always loved art and enjoyed making things. I knew deep down that I wanted my own business whatever that would look like. So, as I went through school (university and after), I pursued many different things. I tried new hobbies, little business ventures, and attempted many different creations. I crafted all through childhood, began making and selling jewellery in my early teens, and I now have a little side hustle of redecorating and styling homes online. I'm grateful to have always been encouraged to try and to do the things that

I love. Regardless of how big or small they become I'm grateful that I have had the faith to **try**. It has been far from perfect but it has been so much fun.

Let me tell you something: You DO NOT have to have all of your ducks in a row to try something new. Without being silly financially or personally, you sometimes just have to go for it and see what happens.

You can't wait for perfection before you try something or you will never start,

whether that be a business, a career, a choice you have to make for your education or a leap into a relationship. Life has its ups and downs, twists and turns, and I have learnt that you have to embrace them and not fight them. You might find some of the best things you do come from those unexpected moments where you took a step towards a goal or stepped out of your comfort zone.

My parents taught me that God's path/plan for your life is not this little narrow road that you have to navigate to keep within his plan. The road to **life** is narrow but what you do with this life is wide and full of opportunities for you to embrace and use for His glory as well as using the gifts and skills that are within you. Embrace the fact that we are all significantly insignificant. We are precious in God's eyes but we are not big or mighty enough to stop His plan or purpose for our lives. He is a good God and, if you follow His leading and direction, you'll not be steered wrong.

Some of you may ask, "But how do I follow His leading?" I have a couple of thoughts that might help you as they have helped me. I know I don't always get it right but I can only recognise and be thankful for where I am—at peace, contented and knowing that I have taken every opportunity that I felt I should have taken. So back to the three things that may help you discern if you are doing what you feel "called" to do or "meant to do."

1. What do you love?

Firstly, am I doing what I love? This could be in relation to a job, a hobby, a side hustle or something you do in your down time. I personally wanted my career to involve something I loved, but I am aware that depending on circumstances that isn't always an option for everyone. If it's not, please don't stop doing what you love. Try to incorporate into your everyday something that you love to do, something that gives you purpose, something that creates that buzz or excitement in you when you get to do it. I think that in church circles the phrase often used as you grow up is to do "what God has called you to do" which then poses the dilemma that most people don't know what that is or don't feel like they have a calling.

Your "calling" as a Christian is to love God and love people.

Your calling is to be an example of love, be there for those in need, care for those around you and seek to grow deeper in your relationship with Jesus. All of us have a calling. At the same time, we can't just go about our lives without aspiring to do something or be somebody, to not only provide for ourselves but for our families, and this is where the confusion comes in.

There can be an expectation that in order to do God's will or calling, you have to serve in ministry within the church or be a missionary in a different country and, of course, there are people called to these things. However, I personally think that perspective (in most cases) couldn't be more wrong. To do what God has called you to do has become over-spiritualised and separated from the "secular" world/everyday living, but when we do that we end up putting God in a box. If you have the Spirit of God living in and working through you, then no matter where you are and what you are doing, people will see His light in you. Jesus isn't confined to the church walls but His Spirit is alive in each one of us as believers.

So when it comes to doing what you love, do it. Whether it is baking, painting, creating, playing a sport, teaching, leading, serving, caring or multiple of the above, do it as if you are doing it for the Lord. The Creator Himself made you with particular talents, skill sets and interests so why wouldn't He want you to use them, and use them for good? Take those things you love and put them into action, do things well, and give God all of the glory.

Something I learnt from the very joy-filled and wise Bob Goff[8] was that to find your purpose or what you are good at is to dig deep into what you really love. "Think about what you did when you were eight years old. What did you do just because it was fun? Take those simple things you did as a kid and embrace them as an adult. Do the things you loved just because you loved them." Sometimes the biggest revelation and most purpose-filled life can come out of embracing those things you loved as a kid. So what was it you loved to do as an eight-year-old?

Does that line up with some of your interests now? Go and do those things.

2. Open doors

Another simple principle I follow when trying to go after God's leading in my life is to open a door and see if it stays open. God has your best interests at heart and wants you to be all He created you to be, using your full potential, so He won't lead you in the wrong direction. Some people get the analogy of the narrow road to faith as being the same narrow road to the perfect plan for your life but as I said previously, I don't believe this is the case. There is one road to life, and that is Jesus, but there is not only one road that you can take in terms of your career or life.

For example, if you like math and love having the opportunity to teach others, you might decide to take a step and apply for university. You pick accounting, economics and teaching. You take the step to apply and leave it to God. You will either get one of your choices and therefore the other doors are closed, you may get more than one offer and then have to choose based on wisdom and discernment, or you may not get any offers in which case I would believe going to university isn't the next immediate step you need to take.

Don't let your emotions override reason but keep opening doors as others close and see what God does. Taking these little steps towards a goal, a career, or a relationship can help you learn to take risks, know it's okay to fail, grow in your trust in Jesus, and learn along the way. Not every step is perfect and not every step is heart-breaking, but you have to make steps in some sort of direction in order for something to happen. So open those doors and if it is for you it will not get past you.

3. Do you have peace in your heart?

Something that needs to coincide with taking steps towards a particular goal is having peace within your heart. Now I'm not talking about a lack of concern because that is expected when you choose to jump towards something or someone worthwhile. However, I am talking about being at peace about a situation, feeling that an opportunity is right not just based off of the facts. Your conscience tends to lead you in the right direction, and having a distinguishing sense between discernment and emotion is key. It's also something that you can determine better over time. So when reaching for goals, starting in a new relationship or deciding to follow a particular career path, make sure you have peace in your heart. Feeling settled in your decision is another clear sign that you are in or following the will of God.

As we go about our lives taking these steps towards doing what we love, meeting new people, learning new things, and taking hold of opportunities, it is important to remember that our Father can and will do exceedingly and abundantly more than we can ask or imagine in all areas of our lives.

In EVERYTHING, God is working, even when we can't see it.

When we do our best and seek to work, serve and love, He is in the midst and working all things for the good of those who love Him. As Paul wrote in Ephesians 3:20, *"Now to Him who is able to do immeasurably more than all we ask or imagine, according to his power that is at work within us, to Him be glory in the church and in Christ Jesus throughout all generations, for ever and ever! Amen."*

He is at work in every situation, He is at work in you, and what He begins He will carry out to completion.

So even when things don't turn out how you expected, He is working, and I can guarantee that most of the time when it doesn't work out it is because He has something better in store for you than you could have imagined or achieved on your own. Worrying about whether you are on the right career path, with the right person or doing the right thing isn't going to get you anywhere, but like I said taking steps towards a passion, an interest or a person will almost always give you your answer as to whether it is for you or not. Some things may not work out how you had planned, you may not be where you think you should be at your age or this stage of life, but you are where you need to be right now, and

God has a purpose for you here and now, no matter how big or small.

In the Bible we can see countless instances where God used unconventional and imperfect people to bring about His plan, whether it was to set people free and bring victory (Rahab, story found in Joshua 2), to be a part of the birth line of Jesus (Book of Ruth), to raise the next generation of God's chosen people (Abraham, Genesis 12-25), to take down a giant (David, 1 Samuel 17) or to deliver God's Word to many (the apostles, The Gospels). Not only did God use people but through His One and only Son Jesus, He redeemed humanity. Jesus established connections and intimacy with people from all walks of life: fishermen, prostitutes, tax collectors, mothers, carpenters, leaders and servants, and through His Spirit to this day we see lives being changed and people being used by Him. Not one of these people mentioned were used in the way in which they thought they would have been. God's use of the unconventional:

OLD TESTAMENT

- God used women to help bring about His plan. In biblical times women were seen as lesser than men, but God saw purpose.
- God helped people to use their talents or skills to bring about victory and miraculous change.
- God used those who were imperfect and ordinary in the sight of the world.

NEW TESTAMENT

- Jesus met people where they were at, regardless of what they had done or where they had been, and He brought about transformation.
- Jesus called imperfect and ordinary people, from tax collectors to fishermen.
- Jesus valued women and also honoured his mother.
- Jesus brought wisdom and change to the way in which humanity worshiped and communicated with the Father. The people thought He came for battle, yet He came for redemption and to save us from our sins.

God is always working, always moving, and always using His people for good. He is not confined to our ideologies, mindsets or situations.

God brings about change and transformation in unconventional ways and, when you are willing, He will use you

—your life, profession, career, conversations, moments, relationships and situations for good and for His glory. We get to be a part of the beautiful tapestry He has woven together called creation.

Trust in His plan even when it doesn't go how you thought it would.

CHAPTER 5
Relationships—Are they important?

When you think about Jesus, what do you think about? Some will think about Him being a baby, Saviour, miracle-worker, Son of God. But have you ever considered that He was a people person? Jesus' entire ministry and life was based on relationships, intimacy and love. He reached out to those in need, built community around Himself and touched the hearts and lives of many who came into contact with Him.

I don't know if you have watched *The Chosen,*[9] but when I heard about this series, I didn't have any urgency to watch it because a lot of the time interpretations of the Bible tend to ad lib and not always portray truth. However, this year I decided to watch Season One on the week leading up to Easter Sunday and it honestly changed me. It doesn't directly follow a specific Bible story but it goes deep into the background of the people of that era, showing the intimacy Jesus had with His disciples and others, and it brings another dimension to the words, actions and intentionality of Jesus. It spoke so deeply to my heart and created an awakening in my understanding and perspective on the beautiful character of Jesus—how He lived and interacted with those around Him.

I am a visual person so watching this series gave me another dimension to the reality and truth of the gospel. I was no longer reading His Word and imagining the era and lifestyle, but I had a visual representation of the time in which Jesus lived. Watching His person displayed as it was in this series brought a stirring in my heart and tears to my eyes. I would encourage you to watch it.

God will and can use ANYTHING to speak to your heart and move your soul. Whether it is reading His Word, talking with a friend, an encounter with a stranger, making dinner or watching a TV program, He is able, He speaks and He is always on the move.

Witnessing Jesus' character come to life in this new way made me want to dig deeper into His story, character and encounters, of which He had many. He had encounters with strangers, companions, His closest friends and family. He valued relationships, and He knew the importance of having them. He knew how much we needed each other as well as the most important relationship of all, our relationship with Him. It is relationships that bring about change and transformation in the lives of others and in our own hearts.

One of my favourite encounters of the New Testament is between Jesus and the Samaritan woman at the well. We read in John 4:5-42 of this encounter and of the personal and larger impact of this meeting. Jesus spoke to this woman with compassion, love, acceptance and mercy, none of which this woman had probably ever experienced before. He asked questions directing conversation towards her reality and sins, yet didn't think any less of her because of them, but accepted her and revealed to her that He, in fact, was the Messiah. Jesus explained that the time had come for true worship and relationship with the Saviour, and it wasn't through buildings or regulations, but it was **in Spirit and Truth** (v23-24). I can't help but feel moved by Jesus' kindness, connecting with someone from a different background and understanding, someone whom others saw as unworthy and dirty, someone that I'm sure felt desperate and hopeless, yet Jesus met her where she was and welcomed her with love. Not only that but (other than the disciples) she was the first person He verbally spoke to about who He was—the beautiful intimacy of Jesus echoing the heart of God, giving humanity hope and establishing the reality that we are both seen and loved.

You don't have to be perfect or strive, you are loved and seen by your Father in Heaven.

You simply have to come humbly before Him with an attitude of repentance and offer Him your life as a vessel. Jesus bought us the ability to have the most beautiful relationship known to man by being redeemed and set free from sin. We have a joy that should enable us to live a life of purpose, devotion and excitement on earth with a hope and assurance of eternal life and peace—to live with an understanding and a trust in Him for the now and beyond, to use our time and possess each day with intentionality for ourselves, for others and most of all for Him.

- How can we begin and use each day to better build our relationship with Jesus?

- How can we take each day to better build our relationship with others?

I hope we can all see that the beauty and purpose of life is found in relationships. Relationships are what make us feel loved, wanted and valued. They are how we can impact those around us, as well as receive intimacy from others. We were built for community, unity and connection, and I believe that truth is displayed the whole way through Jesus' life and ministry and in His love for people.

I think it's clear that the foundation of a good relationship is love. The Bible actually provides four main descriptions of love for us, each one relevant to our different relationships:

Agape — As previously discussed, through Jesus we have the divine love of God, a love that is never ending, unchanging, unexplainable and incomprehensible. This love is like no other. This love is one that accepts you, allows you to come as you are, fully known, fully loved, forgiven and redeemed—a love that sent Jesus, fully God and fully man, to set us free and call us His own—a selfless, beautiful, and life-giving love, the most important love of all. The love our Father in Heaven has for us as His children is unconditional and not determined on what we achieve. It is a relationship with Jesus that brings about change and transformation over regulations, church politics and religion. A relationship with Jesus is one that deals with the condition of the heart, a heart that should be postured towards our Creator.

"For God so loved the world that he gave his one and only Son, that whoever believes in him shall not perish but have eternal life" John 3:16.

Storge — The love that is portrayed through family; a love that has such a deep, unexplainable connection, a sense of belonging, trust and comfort. Family love is one that can't be replaced and is embedded in our hearts forever, the kind of love that allows you to be yourself, not judged, and fully loved. Family is everything. I am so grateful that I am incredibly close with my family. It is something that I truly treasure. If you too are blessed with a family, honour them, be kind, serve and love them, spend time with them, and allow wisdom to be shared and important discussions to be had, in confidence with one another along with having fun, being silly and all of the in between. Family is special. Cherish them.

"Honour your father and your mother, so that you may live long in the land the Lord your God is giving you" Exodus 20:12.

Philia — Brotherly love. The love we have for one another, our friends, companions and neighbours; a love that brings unity, community and adventure; the kind of love that brings people together from all walks of life, with common interests, hobbies, passions or simply the connection created through experiences and being together. This type of love is one that can be built upon over years of experiences and time together. It is also a love that can sometimes happen in an instant with an immediate connection. Brotherly love is so important to build community with larger groups as well as having smaller, intimate relationships with those closest to you, an inner circle of those you can trust and who are sharing the same experiences and walk of life, those in whom you can confide as you go through each season of life. Be sure to build relationship with a few close friends and also connect with others on a different level, showing love and kindness to both those who are like you and those who aren't. Showing love to someone else could change their entire day.

"Be devoted to one another in love. Honour one another above yourselves" Romans 12:10.

Eros — The love most people cherish or long for; a romantic love which is demonstrated through affection, intimacy and acceptance; a type of love that should be celebrated; a love that should have meaning and intentionality; a love that should never be taken for granted. The love shared between a man and a woman is one that is incredibly special; to be there for one another, to trust one another and eventually to unite in marriage, build a life together and become one. Getting to build a life with someone is an incredible gift and a privilege. A union like that should never be taken for granted. I have witnessed many beautiful relationships and have looked on at those who love well. They care for one another, work through difficulties with grace, cheer each other on, and seek to trust God in every area of their lives. Some have displayed to me the beauty of this type of love and been examples of how eros love should be displayed.

"Two are better than one, because they have a good return for their labour: If either of them falls down, one can help the other up. But pity anyone who falls and has no one to help them up" Ecclesiastes 4:9-10.

Love is so beautifully displayed in many ways throughout the Bible and throughout life. It's clear that love has power and when used for the greater good it can be transformative. As we know, love can also be misused and abused but I hope for anyone who may have experienced that type of pain or hurt in their relationships or had a lack of love shown towards them, that through the beautiful sacrifice and life of Jesus, you would know what true love looks like and believe you are loved, and loved unconditionally.

Loving deeply requires sacrifice. It takes time, effort, compromise and adjustment but it also brings joy, companionship, meaning, purpose, connection and comfort.

We were designed for community and built to be there for one another. If not for love, what else connects us? Love is at the core of kindness and should be what drives us to connect, to establish a home, to reach out to those in need, to stop judging, to be hospitable, to serve, to work, to show affection. Everything we do should flow from a place of love. Can you imagine the transformation that would take place in society if we were more intentional in how we love? I know myself that there are moments that I will remember forever where individuals have shown me love through random acts of kindness or in simply being there in moments of sorrow, vulnerability, joy and in different seasons of my life.

Taking into account the questions asked previously in this chapter:

- How do you think that we can show more love to one another in our relationships?

- How can we better build community?

Let's think of ways in which we could love better and build better community. I believe that when we show others who don't think like we do a bit of grace, when we honour our parents, value our families, make new friends, make connections with strangers, take a leap in conversations, and have a bit of fun together, something amazing happens. So let's strive to be more like Jesus in our various relationships and encounters, showing compassion, grace, kindness and, of course, love.

CHAPTER 6
All the single ladies

This is the chapter that I imagine most of you thought the chapter previous was going to be about: romantic relationships. This chapter's focus will be on singleness: how to prepare your heart, how best to use this season of waiting, and to embrace the power and beauty found in being single. So if you have never had a prolonged period of time being single, then this chapter might not resonate with you entirely but I still believe there are truths to be found for you, so please keep reading.

When I was growing up singleness had a bad rap, and a negative light shone on it. It made me think I needed to be in a relationship to be worthy, pretty and part of the group, as a lot of my friends were getting into relationships around their mid to late teens. As I entered into my twenties, I realised quite a few things about the power of singleness and the purpose in being single for a season.

First and foremost, I want to make clear that there have been times that being single has felt lonely and frustrating. You see others around you finding love and getting married and you feel unsure as to why you haven't yet met "the one" or someone who makes you feel special and loved. It can be hard and I totally get it. I know how you feel but believe me when I tell you that once you shift your perspective from pity and transform it to a mindset of opportunity, you won't view singleness in the same way. Loneliness is real, and I can't take that feeling away, but I encourage you to soak yourself in God's Word, surround yourself with good friends and people who love you, find a hobby or something that interests you, and embrace all of this free time you have and the freedom that comes with that.

In order to ease your frustration in singleness, **please stop comparing your life**, especially your love life, to those around you. Instead, think of how you can **use this time effectively**.

So I'm going to get real with you … I don't find it easy to get close to new people. I actually find it really tough. I'm not afraid to talk to or meet new people, but I do **not** like opening up and being vulnerable with someone new, and let me tell you it has been somewhat of a struggle when it comes to dating because of it. My approach to dating (and some other areas in my life) was to appear perfect. I didn't want to allow for silence in conversation, I didn't let them get to know the weird aspects of my personality or my idiosyncrasies, and I felt that being one-on-one with someone meant they were going to analyse everything about me. Since this was my approach when I started dating in my teens, I ended up not letting things go much further than a couple of dates because I freaked myself out about getting close to them. As I look back I know it was completely irrational and that it had nothing to do with the guys. Part of me felt ready to date and be in a relationship because I was in my late teens, and I should have been ready because all of my friends were but, to be honest, I wasn't.

I wanted the image that came with being in a relationship, but I didn't actually want one. I don't know if anyone can relate but it wasn't until I reached a point in my young adult life where I had a period of anxiety and burnout that there was finally a breakthrough in my mindset, my approach and my understanding of not just relationships but of life.

I was finally at a point where I realised that God truly knows me better than I know myself. I went through a period of nearly two years working through some stuff, overcoming worry, dealing with grief, coming to terms with change, and understanding the reality of adulthood. I would love to say that I had a revelation and my mindset was changed overnight but it was actually hard work. Very few people knew what I was going through except my parents and my best friend, and I'm so grateful to them for being there for me in that season. (I encourage you, if you are struggling with anything big or small, please speak to someone—whether a parent or a very close friend—because you don't have to go through things alone.)

When I could no longer keep all of the plates spinning, I came to a place of transformation, my mindset shifted, I focused on things I could control and stepped away from the unrealistic expectation of perfection. So even though this season in my life was a time in which there was a combination of things causing overwhelm, it was in this season that my mindset affected my interaction within dating and relationships.

Now, being a good few years into my twenties I feel like I have learnt a lot through it. I have always been a happy gal who looked at the positive side of life but coming out of those few years of transformation there was a different joy and perspective on adulthood. With that being said, in the midst of that season, one of the many things I learnt was that singleness can be used for good and can be an incredible season of change, growth and development of self-love.

It pains me to see that many young adults are sad that they are single or that they are so lonely that they go after the wrong guy or girl and it causes more harm than good. So I wanted to briefly talk about three things in terms of romantic relationships, love and dating that will hopefully help you if you are in a season of singleness.

You first

This is something that is so important: You need to work on you before you get into a relationship with someone else. None of us are perfect but if you bring your undealt-with insecurities and hurts into a relationship it can create tensions and frustrations that didn't need to be there, and you may end up losing someone who would have been good for you.

During singleness try not to be in a constant state of striving to have or get someone to be a companion for the sake of not being alone.

Use your singleness to grow!

Learn something new, discover a passion, build relationships with those around you, work hard through studies or in your job, spend time with those who are already in your life, invest in areas of life that matter to you, go deeper into your relationship with Jesus, and grow into who you were created to be as an individual **first**.

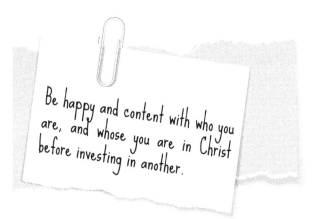

Be happy and content with who you are, and whose you are in Christ before investing in another.

Expectations

This is something that became real for me when I started properly dating, I was comparing a first date to the relationships my friends had when they had been in relationships for a couple of years. I was comparing the conversations to that of a stranger with that of friend which meant I wasn't giving the other person a chance.

There is a danger in expecting perfection from another individual or being in a headspace that you think you need to be perfect for someone else. This can cause a spiral in emotions or cause you to end up in a detrimental relationship rather than a positive one. If you enter into a relationship with an empty or broken heart you will end up jumping into anything, even if it isn't good for you. Don't let your need for someone else outweigh or override your values or disregard the way you should be treated. For example, you may meet someone who says you should act and be a certain way which doesn't line up with your beliefs and character. This could end up altering your perspective, changing what you know to be true and causing conflict and hurt that didn't need to be there to begin with.

So be sure to guard your heart in the process of dating and when getting to know someone new, remove the weight of expectations on yourself and on who you are dating. Lift the pressure, have fun getting to know someone new and be confident in who you are.

No human can or will complete you
This is probably one of the most important things you need to understand when it comes to relationships. NO ONE PERSON CAN OR WILL COMPLETE YOU, so don't expect them to. I have witnessed way too many people searching and longing for a companion in order to feel whole, and the truth is that no one will fill that space inside or the feeling of needing to be loved and accepted other than Jesus. He is the only One that can complete you and fill you. It is an immense amount of pressure to put on another individual if you expect them to make you feel complete or enough.

> A relationship should be the union of two whole people coming together, not two half individuals trying to complete one another.

Relationships are meant to be exciting; they are meant to be where two people connect in such a way that they want nothing more than to be together—two imperfects, yet full in Christ doing their best to love each other and others well.

Relationships have such a beautiful purpose but so does your season of singleness, so don't take it for granted. Being single is the time in your life where you have the most freedom, most disposable income and most free time, so use it wisely in order to better yourself on both the inside and the outside. Don't just seek to survive until you meet the one but THRIVE. Use this time to grow, evolve and become a better version of yourself because as you embrace change you begin to grow, you learn how to respond instead of react, and it enables you to communicate better with others, especially with your other half. So grab this season with both hands, run with it and have fun! Then when you do find your partner, you will already be pursuing, living fully and loving well, and hopefully they will be doing the same. You will be in a frame of mind to easily adapt and make space for one another in each of your lives.

CHAPTER 7
Loss will come

You will always be surrounded by change in life, especially in young adulthood, but it's nearly inevitable in every area of life because you change as you grow. You meet new people, get new jobs, experience new relationships, have new responsibilities, take on new roles and new experiences.

Yet, on top of all of the things you gain and begin to experience, you equally begin to lose things as well. For example, you lose the student life, you lose friendships that you once had, you lose some financial freedom and you will also lose people, for as you get older so does everyone else. I personally don't like to dwell too much on loss, especially with regards to death but it is important to not be blindsided when it comes to this reality of change. Loss can come in many forms: the loss of a time in your life, the loss of a particular ability, the loss of a job, a friend, a family member or the most painful loss of all—death. I briefly want to chat about a couple of areas of loss, those which are really difficult, challenging, sometimes painful and, in a lot of cases, inevitable. Nothing can truly prepare you for loss, but I want to talk you through my experiences in the hope they will offer you some guidance and comfort on your journey.

Where did the structure go?
One aspect of life where you will experience change is in the loss of structure. Right up until this stage of your life everything has been planned out for you. You had school, education, the same yearly layout and the same people around you daily. When all of that is taken away and you are out in the big bad world as some say, it can be scary. If you aren't ready to recognise the reality of this change until you are in it, it can be a time where you might feel a bit lost trying to find your way.

Listen carefully, I'm here to tell you it will be okay. The reality and uncertainty of the changes in your routine, schedule and structure can help you to grow, learn new things, step into more of who you are and what you were meant to do. The change in structure can seem daunting but it gives you freedom to find new hobbies, develop new interests and pursue a career that you truly love. You get more time to develop relationships, spend more time with people, and invest in different areas in your life. In moments of feeling overwhelmed and periods of uncertainty, take one day at a time, one decision at a time and one task at a time.

Don't put too much pressure on yourself. If and when you really don't know which direction to take, remember to look up to the Father. Look up for leading, direction, discernment and a sense of perspective at His creation and ability. If He cares for the wild flowers, how much more does He care for you?

Change of Friendships
Secondly, you will experience the loss of friendships and, in some cases, relationships. When you were a kid or in your teens you most likely had a tightknit group who always had plans to hang out and be with one another, whether it was to do something fun and go on an adventure, sit and watch movies, or keep each other company. I was a part of an amazing friendship group for many years. We went on holidays, spent the entire summers together, we really grew up with one another and were always in each other's company until our twenties. Into adulthood the dynamic of everything changed. Now don't get me wrong, I am still very close with many of those who I grew up with, but the large friendship group that once was, is no longer.

There was a period of time when everyone's schedules changed, personalities developed and grew, things started to change and people drifted apart. There are times I look back and feel sad at the reality of this loss but I couldn't dwell too much on the dynamic that was left behind.

I could only look ahead to who was and what was around me in order to step into another stage of life. I am incredibly grateful for those I do have in my life. I wouldn't be where I am today without those I grew up with but especially without those I have close by my side today.

In seasons of loss no matter how big or small, it can take time to adjust and in this case of loss it can give you space to grow, experience new things and hold tight to those who are in your circle. So whether you have experienced loss/ change in this way or something similar, allow yourself to grow. Allow yourself to be sad at the change whilst being thankful for what once was. Most of all use this change to invest deeply in those around you and to build upon the relationships you do have. The friends you have by your side at this age are those that can last for a lifetime. Cherish them and invest in them. I want to also make clear that when these shifts happen, it normally isn't one person's fault for the separation, for people grow and change. Some stick by each other while others don't. Regardless, **always** cheer each other on and be there for one another even in the midst of uncertain territory and different dynamics.

You may be in a season where you have experienced or are experiencing a toxic relationship. In this case, I also understand the pain that comes with that. I know it's hard to separate yourself because it is comfortable but for your own health and self-worth, step away. Remove yourself from the friendship and allow yourself to find friends who cherish who you are and want to cheer you on, not tear you down.

In both areas of loss within friendships, don't ever doubt your worth, your place or your purpose. Friendship is important and, as you grow and change, so does everyone around you. So be gracious and kind, encourage one another in the victories and comfort one another in times of difficulty. Everyone is on their own journey, some of which you will travel together and others you can cheer on from the side-lines. In loss cherish life and in life cherish friendship.

Grief will come
I now want to talk about grief, which is insanely hard to deal with. With grief, one's body gets hit in a way that is much deeper and emotional than sometimes recognised or realised until the reality sinks in.

My most personal experience of grief was when my grandparents passed away. I knowingly remember the loss of two of my grandparents, and I inwardly miss the two which passed before I was old enough to remember their character but still noticed their absence. I knew as a child that I didn't have either of my grannies present past the age of two, and I was really aware of the fact that others got the chance to see, visit and hug theirs. As I grew up I went through different moments of sadness on the memory of their absence and the reality that I never would get to experience their presence in an earthly way. Whether I knew it or not as a child, there definitely was a void that I began to recognise as an adult. The lack of their presence and input in my life nearly made me grieve them as a grown up even though they were already gone. Yet I got to experience hints towards their character from my parents as I listened to memories and stories of their lives. I also got to look through photos to witness their smiles and beauty.

Then a very present grief surfaced in my late teens when I lost my grandfather and once again in my twenties when I lost the last of my grandparents. The reality and present emotion of loss twice in my young adulthood affected me differently but deeply. When I lost my grandfather back in my teens I was in that place where everything felt like it was shifting, so you can imagine my head was all over the place. I went through a seasonal shift, and it took me several months to start feeling like myself again. I lost not only the man who raised my dad but the man who was always ready to sit with me and watch *The Lion King* and who always encouraged me in my successes. A man of determination and zeal slowly changed and was then promoted to glory. It was only recently that I lost my last grandparent. My grandpa was taken from us in more ways than one—an incredibly difficult deterioration to watch but one that allowed us more time in his presence whether he knew us on not. This man was one that was always present, always cheering me on, came on holidays, was at every occasion and the one I raced with to finish my Sunday dinner every week. Both of these men had a huge impact on my life and on the lives of their families. They walked in faith, stood by God's Word, and loved deeply. I will miss them always, and I am so incredibly grateful for their input into my life.

Talking about these memories is hard but one thing that I would advisee in loss is to allow yourself to grieve, cry, ask questions, be confused and strongly miss who you have lost.

Showing emotion isn't weakness but a way in which you can begin the process of healing.

The people we have or have had in our lives are extremely important and so it makes sense that, when someone is taken away from us, we don't want to be separated. Grief is real, it's tough, it's something that hurts deeply and we can't shy away from that. Time does heal but you will always miss those who are gone and there is still pain in the sorrow.

Yet, even still, in the midst of the sorrow, there is hope. Those who are saved and have accepted Jesus as their Lord and Saviour have the certainty and hope of eternity. Through the blood of Jesus Christ, we have the most beautiful truth that life here on earth is not the end, that there is life after death for all those who believe and have accepted Him as their Saviour. There will be a time of reuniting and of restoring and if that doesn't bring hope I don't know what will.

As you look to the Bible you will see that Jesus was fully man and fully God. He had the divine power of the Father through and within Him but He also knew and experienced the good and bad of human existence simultaneously. The beauty of Jesus is that He brought hope to the hopeless and life to the lifeless. He is the direct connection to the Father, yet He knew what was in the heart and experiences of man. In this we can find comfort in many areas of life, including our losses. Jesus also experienced numerous types of loss. He experienced grief through the death of His friend[10] as well as less severe but still significant losses through the loss of His disciples' attention and presence when He needed them[11] and also his privacy.[12] First and foremost, He lost His life, His earthly body. Yet what seemed hopeless and full of grief turned into the beautiful truth and reality of eternity for Christ followers. **He defeated death**.

The power of the ultimate and most painful loss was broken through the blood of Jesus, bringing about the most hopeful reality of eternity.

This truth of eternity is the only thing that can bring some solace to the loss of a loved one, and it is because of Jesus we have that reality of eternity with Him (for those who have accepted Him as their Lord and Saviour). So in the midst of the pain, sorrow, loss and the unknown, know that Jesus brings comfort and hope. Loss in these different areas of life is inevitable but this much is true: There is hope, there is love and there is a purpose in you and for you in the midst of all the changes, shifts and unknowns.

As everything around you shifts, moves and/or changes, fix your focus on the One who never changes. Like I have said, previously realign and posture yourself towards the Father. Give yourself the time to process the uncertainties in everything we gain and lose as human beings and watch as you grow and learn more about yourself in the process. Most importantly, surround yourself with those who love you well and invest in one another in EVERY season.

CHAPTER 8
STEWARD WELL

I don't know if you have ever heard of the word "stewardship" before or maybe you have heard of it but are unsure what it means. It means, *"The careful and responsible management of something entrusted to one's care."*[13] Taking that into account it is something we should all seek to do well. Whether that be people, money, belongings, careers, or our time and well-being, it's important that we are being intentional and using our time and money effectively whilst looking after our bodies, minds and souls. In every area of our lives, we should seek to be good stewards. This is basically a deeper concept of "caring" and a practical way to better ourselves and those around us.

One of the first things that comes to mind when I hear the word "steward" is money. You have probably heard the phrase, "Money makes the world go around" and, let's be honest, it's kind of true. Without money we wouldn't be able to survive, provide or live. Money makes things possible and, therefore, it is incredibly important that we use money wisely and understand the practical as well as the positive aspects of money.

The Bible is full of knowledge and wisdom on money and how to use it. In fact, did you know that "16[14] out of 38 of Jesus' parables deal with money and possessions"? It is incredibly important in our society, and it is incredibly important to God. That is why I believe it is referenced so often in the Bible. God knew its importance as well as recognising the power money can have positively and negatively. Money can capture and control people to the point of causing detriment to themselves and those around them, but when used correctly money can bring about blessing, provision and change.

By this stage in your life, you are probably already aware of the need for money, the privilege of having your own money, and the responsibilities that come with that. As a young adult, it is the perfect time to get your head around the best ways to use it, invest it and bring honour to God with it.

(Disclaimer: I am not a financial adviser, and these comments are solely my own opinion with reference to Scripture.)

All money is God's money

It is incredibly important to recognise and build your life and finances upon the fact that ALL money is God's money. *"Remember the Lord your God, for it is He who gives you the ability to produce wealth"* Deuteronomy 8:18. When you understand and take this perspective on money, it helps you take the focus off of yourself and onto your provider.

Money is not evil

Another important aspect of money is to acknowledge that money itself isn't evil but the love of money is. *"For the love of money is a root of all kinds of evil and by craving it, some have wandered away from the faith and pierced themselves with many griefs"* 1 Timothy 6:10. Money can be powerful in both positive and negative ways depending on how you use it and view it. An obsession with money to the point of greed and overconsumption is what causes destruction. With that being said, an overconsumption of anything other than Jesus can have its detrimental and negative effects. Something else that is important to note is that the love of money is not just applicable to those with great wealth, but the love of money can be seen in anyone regardless of what is in the bank account. It is a condition of the heart.

Recognising the importance of money, who your money belongs to and the power of money gives you an incredible starting point to then filter into **how you use** your money, how to use it **wisely** and to the best of your ability. This new independent stage of life brings more responsibility, and some of the things you have to start thinking about include budgeting, taxes, bills, giving, investing and stewarding your money well. Dealing with money is one of the many things that come along with adulthood and is also one of the biggest challenges to manage and use well.

Taking these concepts on board I believe it would be useful to look at three areas of thought surrounding how we can steward well. Firstly, in terms of money and then looking at stewardship with regards to time.

MONEY

Giving

Giving is one of the most well-known ways in which the Bible explains how to use our money. Whether giving to others, to the church, to the needy or to particular causes—all are important and beneficial. The Bible also makes it clear that we should not give with reluctance, and you shouldn't feel the need to show off to others about your giving. *"Each of you should give what you have decided in your heart to give, not reluctantly or under compulsion, for God loves a cheerful giver"* 2 Corinthians 9:7. So whether you can give a little or a lot is not a concern to God; it's how you give and with what attitude you distribute your cash. Giving back to God, or tithing, is an Old Testament biblical action; however, it is still incredibly important today. Going back to the understanding that all money is God's money gives another perspective to the reason and joy of being able to give back. Whether to the church or to people, giving your money back to God is a sign of honour and acknowledgment of His sovereignty.

Investing

This is an interesting one, and I know it can be taken in different ways by different people but whilst taking the focus off of the somewhat grey area on short-term investments, let's look at the importance and usefulness surrounding long-term investments.[15] "Investment can be defined as putting your money into financial schemes, shares, property or ventures with the expectation of achieving a profit"[16] or "devoting your time, effort and energy into a particular undertaking with the expectation of a worthwhile result." So whilst taking into account these two aspects of investing, both similarly are to achieve a positive result or profit in some way.

This leads me onto my perspective and belief in the importance of financially investing. If we are to build our lives upon Jesus, have Him in the midst of every decision and filter Him into every area of our lives, then why would we invest in people, relationships and our careers but not our finances? The parable of the talents is one that I always refer to as an example of investing. You can interpret this passage in terms of finances and also in terms of your skills (anything in your life that will increase as you spend time and effort working towards).

"For it will be like a man going on a journey, who called his servants and entrusted to them his property. To one he gave five talents to another two, to another one, each according to his ability. Then he went away. He who had received the five talents went at once and traded with them, and he made five talents more. So also he who had the two talents made two talents more. But he who had received the one talent went and dug a hole in the ground and hid his master's money. Now after a long time the master of those servants came and settled accounts with them. "And he who had received the five talents came forward, bringing five talents more, saying, 'Master, you delivered to me five talents; here, I have made five talents more.' His master said to him, 'Well done, good and faithful servant. You have been faithful over a little; I will set you over much. Enter into the joy of your master.' And he also who had the two talents came forward, saying, 'Master, you delivered to me two talents; here, I have made two talents more.' His master said to him, 'Well done, good and faithful servant. You have been faithful over a little; I will set you over much. Enter into the joy of your master.' He also who had received the one talent came forward, saying, 'Master, I knew you to be a hard man, reaping where you did not sow, and gathering where you scattered no seed, so

I was afraid, and I went and hid your talent in the ground. Here, you have what is yours.' But his master answered him, 'You wicked and slothful servant! You knew that I reap where I have not sown and gather where I scattered no seed?" Matthew 25:14-26.

Investing in many areas of life is important. It creates purpose and intentionality whilst preparing and planning for the future.

Going back to financial investments, I believe it can be wise to put your money into long-term funds or projects in order to prepare for the future and help you to begin to build a stable portfolio of income. This will give you more money to then invest back into your home, your family, your church, to give to others and to give you the opportunity to do many great things and create positive change for those around you.

Providing

This leads into my last point on the positives surrounding the use of our money, and that is to provide. Like I said above, one way of providing for yourself and others is investing but your job and other ventures are also a couple of ways to bring money your way and allow you to filter into the various aspects of life. *"Invest in seven ventures, yes in eight: you do not know what disaster may come upon the land"* Ecclesiastes 11:2. One of the main reasons we earn our money is to allow us to provide for our families, ourselves and those closest to us. What a privilege and honour to be able to provide for your partner, your kids, and those around you. *"But if anyone does not provide for his relatives, and especially for members of his household, he has denied the faith and is worse than an unbeliever"* 1 Timothy 5:8. Having money to provide and the ability to provide shouldn't be overlooked. It is important, biblical and special.

Money is a tool and, when used wisely, biblically and practically, it can be an incredible blessing. *"Whoever brings blessing will be enriched and one who waters will himself be watered"* Proverbs 11:35.

TIME

Giving

It's been said that giving is better than receiving, and I have to say that I love a bit of both. I love getting presents wrapped up for those I love as well as still being that adult who gets excited for Christmas morning. Isn't it funny that we get excited to give and receive "stuff"? And don't get me wrong: That element of giving is great, especially if your love language is "receiving gifts." Yet I want to direct your attention a different way when it comes to giving. What would it mean for us to give of our time? Time is SO precious and it is incredibly important that we use our time wisely. Giving of our time could look like meeting a friend for coffee, setting time aside from work to play with your kids, working towards a promotion or goal, it could be a number of things—each one different to you and me. Whatever way you feel led to give of your time, you should seek to make intentional steps in that direction.

In Hebrews 13:16 it says, *"Do not forget to do good and to help one another, because these are the sacrifices that please God"* (GNT). Helping one another and being there for one another is pleasing to God so take a look at who is around you and think of one way in which you could give of your time to better someone else or spread some goodness.

Investing

Investing in other people goes hand in hand with giving to others. Giving of your time helps us to better those around us, not just for that moment but for relationships to be built, community to be formed and to have a lasting impact on those we have around us. Investment is essential to living a fruitful life. 2 Corinthians 9:6 says, *"The person who sows sparingly will also reap sparingly, and the person who sows generously will also reap generously"* (CSB). So in order to reap you have to sow, you have to take action and show kindness, have deep conversations with those you trust, talk to that stranger, pray with your kids, study hard to pursue your career, and start to take responsibility of your time.

As I said above, investing in many areas of your life creates purpose and intentionality now whilst preparing and planning for the future. So use your time wisely and invest in the things that matter.

Providing

Finally, how can we use our time to provide? It's the same concept as with money. We give and invest in order to provide. These three points all require action and as you seek to give more of your time and invest your time in things that matter, it leads to the process of providing—providing kindness to the hurting, solace to the broken-hearted, joy to those burdened, a happy home for your family and words of encouragement to build one another up. It's all of these simple things that bring us together as human beings and, if we were to just use our time more intentionally for one another, can you imagine the transformations that could take place in people's hearts and lives? More people would feel and know they are loved and wanted.

Of course, none of the above would have the same purpose and significance if it wasn't for Jesus. It is through Him and because of Him that we have hope and purpose. He is what gives our lives meaning, and He knows we need each other too.

So let's take some actionable steps towards stewarding our lives well and living with intentionality in each area of our lives!

(P.S. Don't forget to look after yourself, to steward well for your own well-being too. You have to take the time to invest in your own mental and physical health in order to effectively live out the life you were called to live. We will talk more about that in the next chapter.)

CHAPTER 9

Consumption

As I stated earlier, an overconsumption of anything other than Jesus can be detrimental to your health, whether that be mental, physical or spiritual. What you consume and how much you consume is important and affects you both internally and externally. You could look at every area of your life as an example: what you eat, how much you exercise, what you look at, how you engage with others, your money, buying habits, attitude, and how you carry yourself—all of which are affected by how much or how little effort you put towards them and that then has its many effects on you.

If we first talk about our minds, the most powerful and intricate organ and part of the body from which everything else flows, the part of the body that allows us to think, gives us the ability to move, and allows us to have deep connections with others.

> If everything we do comes from within and our actions are based off of our thoughts, then should we not be really intentional about what we put into our minds?

I believe that what we watch, what and who we listen to and what we read has a deeper interaction internally and with our souls than I sometimes think we realise.

If you are in a toxic relationship that is constantly tearing you down and making you feel worthless or if you are repeatedly watching something you know you shouldn't and it's impacting your interactions and relationships with others, then maybe it is time to change some of your routines or habits. What we put into our minds will eventually be what comes out. If our thoughts become inundated with negativity, hurtful comments, misuse of power, aggravation, anger, over-sexualised romance or violence, then it can begin to be what you believe, think and know. This can then filter into how we act, impact our attitude, bring fluctuations to our character and affect how we treat others.

Having any form of media at our fingertips and sharing information about ourselves and others daily can begin to leave room for comments of hate, comparison and a lot more to flood in. No wonder so many have trouble concentrating, sleeping or staying on top of their game, especially if their intention is to receive validation from others.

In order to combat all the things this world throws at us through its many sources of media and communication as well as the negativity that comes from others, there needs to be a source of light to breathe hope and wisdom into all circumstances, and I believe that hope is Jesus. One of the most effective ways to combat the negativity of the world is to engross yourself in the Word of God. The more you consume His Word and soak in His goodness, the more you will experience and begin to recognise the inward transformation taking place, where His Word will breathe life and light into the unknown and uncertain times.

It's also incredibly important to surround yourself with the right people. Through our screens and conversations, it is important to take in information that is of value and builds you up. Follow people who inspire you and build friendships with people who encourage you and show you love. There is great importance in surrounding yourself with the right people. The "right people" will be honest, seek your best and lift you up. So seek to surround yourself with those that show you that kind of love.

Who you hang out with is who you become! Think about who you hang out with, for you deserve to be shown love and kindness.

> You need to realise that you were made for more. You were created with purpose and built with intention.

So instead of taking on the world and all of its problems, look at the world through new lenses and see it for its beauty, its opportunities, and its value. Simply spreading a bit of love and kindness or looking at the landscape or up to the sky can put life into perspective in how BIG and how good God is.

Time out and looking up to the heavens can shift your gaze from your current situation to the One who is above, recognising that if God cares for the birds in the sky[17] and holds the oceans in place[18] while keeping us from getting dizzy as the world spins on its axis,[19] then He most definitely cares, holds and keeps YOU. YES YOU, MY FRIEND!

Let the overconsumption of what the world tries to throw at you be replaced by the Word of God and meaningful relationships. Begin to fill your mind with things of value.

With that in mind, what we consume mentally is not the only area of consumption we need to be aware of, but we need to be intentional about what we put into our physical bodies. Our body is a temple and, therefore, we should treat it as such. I know at times you may not feel like it or believe it, but you were made in the image of God, so you have got to start acting like it. We should give our bodies the appropriate care and love in the same way we care about making money. It should be a priority to look after your health and your physical body at every stage of your life, for it has an impact upon the next stage.

If this last year or so has taught us anything, it is that we are allowed to slow down, take a breather and rest. We are a part of an incredibly fast-paced world, and it wasn't until the world technically stopped that we finally stopped. People were able to spend more time with their families, pursue once-old passions, create businesses, and get more into fitness. In the midst of the heartache and confusion we were given a gift. As a generation, we were able to take a step back and assess our lives, our purposes, and really be intentional about what we do, who we surround ourselves with, and how we use our time.

So whether you were one of the people to have taken up a hobby and made it a career, whether you became more intentional with what you ate and how you treated your body or whether you were someone who really struggled and just spent the time reading, sitting, pondering and dreaming, now is the time to be intentional. Now is the time to take account of what you consume, how much you consume, and how it is affecting you, your health and your abilities.

For me, I have tried to be more intentional with my time in general. I have (surprisingly) got myself into a routine of working out. I wanted to try to make exercise a habit and become something I enjoyed rather than dreaded and I'm so proud to say I did. I'm not joking when I say it has made me feel so much better. I have more energy for the day, I have more confidence in my body, I'm proud of my ability and what my body can do. I feel more focused, I get fewer headaches and it has made me healthier as a whole, both mentally and physically. How we physically treat our bodies also has a massive effect on our minds—the physical impacts the mental and vice versa. In fact, the National Institute of Health stated that exercise can increase the production of endorphins which are known to help produce positive feelings and reduce the perception of pain.[20] So the more we look after our bodies, the more we are looking after our mental wellbeing too.

Going back to what I said before, what we put into our bodies and minds can be transformative, and it is dependent on you as to what end of the spectrum you want to be on. I know there are many factors that can filter into our decisions and lifestyles but simply taking one step in either direction tends to gain traction towards a certain way of life. If you tell yourself you are going to get up half an hour earlier every morning and you are determined to stick to it, then it will eventually become a habit that could lead to you having that time for exercise or to read and meditate before you start your day. Whereas, if you make a decision to put on a new series at 11:00 p.m. (guilty lol), you most likely won't be well rested for the next day.

> Decisions we make become
> habits we keep.

I encourage you to take one step or one action towards being more intentional with your time and allow it to be something that will fill your mind, body and soul with something positive, beneficial and encouraging. Those habits that you embed in your everyday, whether spiritually, physically or mentally will impact your life more than you know. Look after your body, mind and soul. Use your being as a vessel for good and for God.

CHAPTER 10
Let's have fun

Those who know me know that I am one of those obsessive dog mums and my little pup is like my baby. Honestly, you only understand the true love and connection with a dog and the comfort, joy and fun that you get from their presence once you have your own. I can't help but compare the imagery to that of us towards God. I believe we can see the character, beauty and presence of God in almost anything if we look for it, and one of those things for me would be in the relationship between owner and dog.

My dog comes to my feet for attention and cuddles. He lets me know when he needs food or water and when he wants to have fun and play. My attitude towards him no matter the reason for his pine, is to help him, be with him and be close to him. Does that not sound familiar to us in communication with God? We come to Him and speak to Him for what we need and want and simply to be in His presence, and God wants nothing more than to just be with us.

He doesn't expect us to be everything;
instead, He wants us to come to Him,
for Him to be our everything.

So come to the Father to enjoy His presence, experience His comfort, embrace His love, be filled with His joy and have fun.

Some of you may be thinking, what do you mean have fun? This is something that I would love for you to grasp and embrace as you grow into your adulthood: NEVER FORGET TO HAVE FUN. Allow your inner child to come out in your everyday. Just because you are physically older doesn't mean you have to become boring. Throughout your teens, you tend to become more aware and scared about what people think of you, and your confidence can become shaken by the comments of others, but I want you to know that your confidence can be found in Him. When it does, that inner confidence found in the One who holds it all will cause an overflow of joy and hope. Allow that joy and hope to take away the fear of having fun, being silly, or caring what people think of you.

As a kid you most likely had the gumption to try anything, have fun, play games, go on adventures, and just enjoy the little moments. Bring back that part of you, not bringing with it immaturity and lack of wisdom, but bring back your childlike freedom and light-heartedness to life again. So much that happens around us can be confusing, overwhelming and uncertain but we can choose to look for the good, rejoice, embrace opportunities and enjoy life because we have a God who holds our tomorrows.

Have you ever been asked, "If you could have dinner with three people—dead or alive—who would they be?" Think about that for a moment. What three people—dead or alive—would you love to have dinner with?

For me, there is one man who I would love to have a conversation with, and it is Bob Goff. He is a man who oozes life, joy and fun every time I listen to him speak or read his books, I find myself smiling at his expression and exuberance for life. He finds joy in everything and anything and really believes in the power of love—the love of God and the power in us to love others. A clear example of the joy he has for life is evident in the fact that he has an office and holds business meetings in Disneyland and he went skydiving with his son on a whim. So if you are looking for ways to bring some fun into your everyday, listen to Bob Goff.

As adults we tend to forget to have fun, whether it's the added responsibilities, trying to be cool or project a certain image, or you might just forget how to. But if you lose fun, you slowly begin to lose laughter and joy in the silly things, and you end up missing out on so much. My mum is someone who has never forgotten how to have fun, embracing every moment and dancing like no one is watching. I remember as a kid we were in a shopping centre and there was a catwalk for a fashion show a few days later, and we were joking about getting up to do a walk down the catwalk but to mum it wasn't just an idea. She went and strutted her stuff down the catwalk. I was so embarrassed but looking back I am glad that my mum showed me that you can have fun at any age. To this day she continues to display so much joy and fun in everything she does, and I am glad I have her to not only look up to but to enjoy those fun moments with. A little motto to live by written by Chris Tomlin and one which my mum recites all of the time is, *"Live like there's no tomorrow, dance like no one's around, sing like nobody's listening, give like you have plenty, and love like you're not afraid."*[21]

Whether you have someone to show you what it means to have fun or not, I am telling you it's okay to have fun and I am telling **you** to be the example to others by having fun. Like I said before, adulthood can sometimes be really tough but don't make it harder than it needs to be by being serious all of the time.

We need some young adults to start spreading some joy and sprinkling moments of fun into adulthood rather than trying so hard to act like grownups.

Something that has stuck with me from the moment I watched it is a scene towards the end of *Mary Poppins Returns*.[22] (Nothing like a Disney movie to bring some inspiration) The scene begins with the children arriving at a funfair with their father. Minutes before, he had just had a breakthrough which caused his attitude of seriousness and constant worry to change. If you have seen it, then you know as they enter the fair they spot balloons for sale, and the lady selling them told the father to choose carefully. It was only then that he realised he hadn't held one since he was a child. She said, "Then you have forgotten what it is like?" He responded, "To hold a balloon?" ... "*No. To be a child.*"

He had forgotten what it was like to be a child, to hold a balloon and look up at its simplistic beauty, and the excitement that came from receiving one. For you, that might sound simple or silly but sometimes the simplest of things can bring about the most change, even the simple act of deciding to have fun, learning to laugh at yourself and not take yourself too seriously, enjoying life.

I hope and pray that, within each stage of your life, you will never forget to look up. Look up to your Creator, look to His creation for a newfound perspective on His vastness and love. When you look up as a child looks up to a balloon in the sky, look up with hope, anticipation and joy for all that God can accomplish and do through you, as well as looking up with thankfulness and gratefulness for who He is and all He has done. So go and HAVE FUN, try something new, challenge yourself and allow those simple moments to transform not only your day but your perspective.

CHAPTER 11
JUST BE

As a young adult you will soon realise that you become constantly bombarded with people telling you that you need to figure out who you are, what you love, what you want to do, and where you want to go in life. It can be exhausting. You get to a stage where you are that busy trying to figure out what you want to study, do as a career or pursue, that you actually forget to think about what you really love and zone in on **who you are** and not just on what you do or want to do. But please do not miss out on where you are at right NOW by being so busy trying to do or be the next thing.

Society has engrained in us that we constantly need to be striving and, in a lot of cases, to the point of rushing past the present moment in order to reach the next step or next stage in life. Yet, if you keep yourself in that attitude of eagerness for what's next and seek to constantly be onto the next thing, you will forget to live in the here and now. I know so many people who need to have something grasping their attention to be happy, but all it's doing is distracting you from living in the moment, causing you to miss out, or helping you to avoid the reality of today while wishing for a different circumstance. I literally plead with you: Don't miss out on today. Live in the "now" and stop trying to rush every stage of your life. You could end up missing some incredible moments.

Now don't get me wrong, even though being present is key, doing something with your time is also essential and wise. Part of life, especially this stage of life, is to find a job or career, to pursue it and do it well. I totally agree with the need to work and to work hard in order to earn a living and know what it is to earn or achieve something. There is great importance in that, and I am a true advocate of pursuing your passions and finding a job that you love. I believe you have those passions and talents inside of you for a reason. God put those skills in you with intentionality and for a greater purpose as well as for the joy of doing.

However, I want to dig deeper into the fact it isn't all about doing but about being. First and foremost, you are a human being. Even though we DO things such as work, serve others, love deeply and socialise, in the words of Arielle Estoria,[23]"We are not known as human DOINGS but HUMAN BEINGS." You are filled with incredible and significant purpose just by being a human on this earth. You are here for a reason. You have purpose. You are enough, and you are worthy just as you are without having to *do* anything.

Take in this beautiful truth that comes from the Father: *"I have called your name, you're mine"* (Isaiah 43:1 MSG). Our Father in Heaven loved you before you had achieved anything, He loves you simply because you are His creation. He loves you and is proud of you.

So in the hustle and bustle don't get too caught up in it all that you miss the beauty in your human being-ness.

With that, I want to share one of the most beautiful passages of Scripture with you. I want you to read it slowly, digest the words, and embrace the truth of what is written and know it was written with YOU in mind:

"You have searched me, Lord, and you know me. You know when I sit and when I rise; you perceive my thoughts from afar. You discern my going out and my lying down; you are familiar with all my ways. Before a word is on my tongue you, Lord, know it completely. You hem me in behind and before, and you lay your hand upon me. Such knowledge is too wonderful for me, too lofty for me to attain. Where can I go from your Spirit? Where can I flee from your presence? For you created my inmost being; you knit me together in my mother's womb. I praise you because I am fearfully and wonderfully made; your works are wonderful, I know that full well. My frame was not hidden from you when I was made in the secret place, when I was woven together in the depths of the earth. Your eyes saw my unformed body; all the days ordained for me were written in your book before one of them came to be. How precious to me are your thoughts, God! How vast is the sum of them! Were I to count them, they would outnumber the grains of sand. When I awake, I am still with you"
Psalms 139:1-7, 13-18.

It's not often that we are praised or congratulated on just being ourselves. More often than not it's when you achieve something, get a job, buy a house, get engaged or complete your studies. These are all things that should be celebrated but don't miss out on the reality that you should be celebrated because you are you. We all have different personalities, traits and quirks, and all of them (some coming with their challenges) make us who we are. That's something that should be embraced and cherished. Even when people are difficult it's time to show a little bit of grace and compassion to the fact that we are all human, all different and yet all loved.

For a long time, I struggled to get my head around the fact that I was enough by just being me. I understood and believed that Jesus loved me regardless of what I achieved or did but I lived so much of my life for other people, trying to please them and be perfect. A lot of this perspective was due to my analytical thought process but there were many comments, conversations and scenarios that happened in my teens that planted the seeds of this expectation of perfection in my head. I felt that I wasn't allowed to show if I had a bad day or wasn't feeling one hundred percent. In order to achieve a sense of excellence in what I was doing it meant meeting other people's expectations and, a lot of the time, it was unachievable.

As I explained earlier, when I was in that season of anxiety and constant change, I let it affect not only my mindset but my relationships. I had begun to put so much pressure on myself to be perfect that two things happened: I became so overwhelmed with doing everything (at times what felt like for everyone else) I experienced burnout, and I also began to become weary of being vulnerable and opening up to people because I didn't want to come across the wrong way or be interpreted wrongly.

Overwhelmed

The main reason I became so overwhelmed was because I just couldn't say no. I said yes to everything I was asked to be a part of, serve in and do and, as a young teen, you have that much enthusiasm and time that it comes as a privilege to do all of those things. However, when you start to get more responsibilities, your studies become more intense, along with all of the things you are a part of and begin to experience it can become overwhelming. You end up having no time for yourself or your family. I ended up being at a stage in my life where I was lucky to get one night a week in the house without running to church, being a part of a small group, studying, revising for exams or preparing for certain events. I was trying hard to please everyone and, in a way, prove myself, that I ended up dropping all of the plates I was trying to keep spinning and, therefore, experienced burnout. I felt awful, and it took me getting to that point of breakdown/burnout before I did something about it.

Vulnerability

I also began to be more aware of my interactions with people. It became an issue not only with meeting new people but also with those I had known for a long time, as if I was trying to prove something to them—all because of this expectation of perfection and aiming for such a high standard, an understanding that it was all based around what I could do and how much I could do. And let me tell you, if you focus too much on doing over just being, you won't be able to keep on doing.

If you are at a stage in life where you feel overwhelmed, bogged down, worried or exhausted, it's time to take steps of intentionality towards or away from certain things and allow yourself time to rest and **just be**. For so long I had seen "rest" as a weakness or a bad thing. Having a day off meant I had a free day to do more work. The fact is that you need days off, you need days for yourself to do things you love just because you love it. You need days to just be and rejuvenate your soul.

If God saw rest as holy, then I think it is something we need to make time for. *"In the beginning God created the heavens and the earth, day after day He spoke creation into existence and on the seventh day He rested, He called it good and HOLY"* Genesis 2:2. Don't take for granted your time to rest, because without it you won't be as effective in your doing.

When your **being** isn't getting refreshed and refuelled, your **doing** becomes stressful and strained. So please make sure you take some time for yourself, to rest and to spend time doing what you love with those you love.

A beautiful example in the Bible depicting an lifestyle of rest is when Jesus comes to Mary and Martha's home. *"As Jesus and his disciples were on their way, he came to a village where a woman named Martha opened her home to him. She had a sister called Mary, who sat at the Lord's feet listening to what he said. But Martha was distracted by all the preparations that had to be made. She came to him and asked, 'Lord, don't you care that my sister has left me to do the work by myself? Tell her to help me!' 'Martha, Martha,' the Lord answered, 'you are worried and upset about many things, but few things are needed—or indeed only one. Mary has chosen what is better, and it will not be taken away from her'"* Luke 10:38-42.

Now I don't know about you, but I can relate to Martha, being the busy bee and making sure everything is organised, but I don't think the fact that Martha was busy and Mary wasn't is the main takeaway from these verses. I think it is more about the direction of their attention.

There was nothing wrong with Martha getting the food ready because at the end of the day they needed to eat, yet for Mary her gaze was so fixed on Jesus, overcome that He was in their midst she couldn't help but sit at His feet. Her priority was to just be in the presence of her Saviour. Whilst Martha was in the hustle of preparing the food and serving she still was doing it with purpose and in recognition that Jesus was in her midst. The only difference was that one was working from a place of striving to please God instead of being still in the presence of God.

Life is normally quite busy. It is good to serve, and it's important to not lose sight of the importance of those tasks. But your foundation of DOING should not come from a place of busyness leading to distraction. It should instead be from a place of rest and peace, built upon the foundation of God's promises and presence.

The earlier you grasp that it is all about Jesus and His work in us, the quicker your focus will shift from yourself and your expectation to be _____ (in my case "perfect"). Then you can find your confidence and freedom in who HE is and who HE is in you instead of relying on your own strengths, achievements and abilities. Once you get to that place of complete confidence in your Creator and your gaze is fixed on Him, you begin to realise that He loves you irrespective of your achievements, your performance or your profession. He simply loves you for being you. Jesus was brought to earth over 2,000 years ago so that not only then but now, we could and can live in freedom. We can have a sense of inner peace. We have the ability to be happy and contented where we are at. Jesus gives us hope, and His love allows us to just be.

"For God so loved the world that he gave his one and only Son, that whoever believes in him shall not perish but have eternal life" John 3:16. A love that is beyond comprehension. A love that meets us where we are, as we are and calls us His own. A love that broke the barrier between God and man, tore the veil in two, uniting us with **His presence** both now and forever. The beautiful life, death and resurrection of Jesus created the most intricately woven tapestry of love from the beginning of creation.

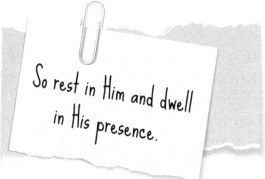

So rest in Him and dwell in His presence.

I really hope that as you have read through this book, you have learnt something new or been reminded of something that has helped you to grasp and understand your purpose in Christ, your worth and some wisdom surrounding the changes and practicalities of young adulthood.

Don't forget to lift your eyes to the one who is in all, above all and through all.
Embrace His presence.
Be intentional with your life.
Spend time with those you love.
Follow your passions.
Show the love and kindness of Jesus to those around you.
Trust the process.
Navigate the changes with the certainty that your Heavenly Father is with you.
Remember He has got you right in the palm of His hand.

It's time to look up!

Endnotes

1   Set of fantasy novels by Northern Ireland C.S. Lewis.
2   https://en.wikipedia.org/wiki/Footprints_(poem)
3   Lauren Daigle, Look Up, Child, Franklin, Tennessee: Centricity Music (2018).
4   Not Forsaken, Author Louie Giglio, published by Lifeway Christian Resources, 2019
5   Matthew 7:8-11
6   https://tlexinstitute.com/how-to-effortlessly-have-more-positive-thoughts/
7   Holman, Raechel Myers, Amanda Bible Williams, CBS She Reads Truth Bible, Broadman & Holman Publishers (2019).
8   Best-selling author and speaker Bob Goff, 12th September 18 [WHOA That's Good Podcast], 12 September (2018). Available at https://podcasts.apple.com/us/podcast premiere-episode-bestselling-author-speaker-bob-goff/ id1433974017?i=1000419574492 (Accessed: 20/05/2020)
9   www.thechosen.tv/app
10   John 11.1-45
11   Matthew 26.40
12   Matthew 26.40
13   https://www.merriam-webster.com/dictionary/stewardship
14   Tithe.ly, Bible verses about money: 9 biblical principles of money & possessions, (2020). Viewed: 20/05/2020. Link: https://get.tithe.ly/blog/bible-verses-about-money.
15   Dictionary, Investment, result 1 (2020). Viewed: 20/05/2020. Link: https://www.dictionary.com/browse/investment
16   Dictionary, Investment, result 6 (2020). Viewed: 20/05/2020. Link: https://www.dictionary.com/browse/investment
17   Matthew 6:26-34
18   Isaiah 40:12
19   Psalms 24:1-2
20   https://www.healthline.com/nutrition/10-benefits-of-exercise Healthline.com
21   Chris Tomlin, Indescribable, Atlanta: sixstepsrecords (2008).
22   Mary Poppins Returns
23   Arielle Estoria, Unstoppable Year by Bethany Hamilton (2019). Viewed: 20/05/2020. Link:https://www.youtube.com/watch?v=XVCLVdN0BrY

CONTACT
To contact author, get in touch via this email
erinlgraylookup@yahoo.com

Inspired to write a book?

Contact
Maurice Wylie Media
Your Inspirational Christian Publisher

Based in Northern Ireland and distributing
around the world

www.MauriceWylieMedia.com

Lightning Source UK Ltd.
Milton Keynes UK
UKHW021638071221
395235UK00005B/43

9 781915 223029